ARF YA'
B 5

GW00703509

LEE BOK

Crombie Jardine

PUBLISHING LIMITED

13 Nonsuch Walk, Cheam, Surrey, SM2 7LG

www.crombiejardine.com

This edition was first published by
Crombie Jardine Publishing Limited in 2006

ISBN 1-905102-75-5

Written by Michael Powell

Designed by Stewart Ferris
Cover illustration by Rob Smith

Printed by William Clowes, Beccles, Suffolk

CONTENTS

10 REASONS NOT TO PRACTISE SAFE SEX

1. It's easier to swallow than go to the bathroom for a tissue.
2. You can't catch HIV because you're not gay.
3. Condom packaging is too fiddly.
4. Your sister's boyfriend has had the snip.
5. You're already HIV positive, and you can't get it twice.
6. You always pay extra for pink on pink.
7. You've never caught a disease from a hamster.

8. Vaginal warts are ribbed for your pleasure.
9. You always pull out and jizz on her back.
10. The only dangerous part of your lovemaking is digging up the body.

10 REASONS NOT TO HAVE CHILDREN

1. They give you stretch marks and say the stupidest crap you've ever heard in your life.
2. The little shits throw tantrums when you don't buy them toys and cigarettes.
3. You don't want to be a grandparent before you're thirty.
4. Your boyfriend always pays for your abortions.
5. You just had your boobs done.
6. Eventually they all get taken into care.

7. Your dad doesn't want any more children.
8. Prisons are already overcrowded.
9. Screw the earth – *you* have finite resources.
10. You don't need anyone else giving you evils.

10 REASONS NOT TO THINK POSITIVELY

1. Positive people are annoying as hell. When something really shitty has happened and you just want to wallow in your own worthlessness, they always trot out platitudes like "there's plenty more fish in the sea" or "it just wasn't meant to be" or "maybe it's for the best". Arrrgghhh.
2. It's pseudo mind-fooling crap which helps sad losers tolerate their miserable pointless lives.
3. If you think the worst, you can never be disappointed.

4. Why should someone starving in Africa think positively – exactly – proving that it's a decadent up-your-arse Western way of dealing with the world when life gets too comfortable.

5. Thinking the best of people gets you screwed over every time.

6. Shit happens, regardless of whether you are thinking happy thoughts; life really sucks most of the time – deal with it.

7. *X-Factor* auditions: Ten thousand wannabe twats who are living proof that thinking positively about your worse than meagre abilities a) makes you look a twat b) wastes everybody else's time c) turns you

into fodder for exploitation TV culture.

8. Maybe if Americans weren't so goddam smiley smug positive all the time they would look around them and realize that they've destabilized the Middle East, they are stopping the rest of the world from saving the planet, their president is a complete retard and everybody hates them.

9. Behind every cloud the sun is shining – yeah, but you can't see it because there a friggin' great cloud in the way.

10. Jesus was one of the most positive people who ever lived, and look what happened to him.

5 REASONS NOT TO TRAVEL ABROAD

1. Tolerance is one of your best qualities, which is why you don't want to waste it on foreigners.
2. Old people abroad have practically no teeth.
3. It's stupid to travel abroad to fight; it distracts you from the important job of convincing the foreigners who are here to go home.
4. Foreigners are even more fanatical about football than you are.
5. Foreigners are just immigrants who were too poor to escape their own country.

10 REASONS NOT TO HELP AN OLD LADY WHO HAS FALLEN OVER IN THE STREET

1. She's probably had a heart attack, and anything you try to do will make it worse. A little knowledge is a dangerous thing. Best leave it to the professionals.

2. Her time was up; who are you to interfere with God's divine purpose?

3. She's bound to have pissed herself, and you'll be expected to take your

jumper off and put it under her head, and then the piss will start oozing across the pavement towards your jumper and you won't be able to take your eyes off it, and you'll be so busy hoping you don't get piss on your clothes you won't jump out of the way fast enough when some do-gooder rolls her stinking carcass into the recovery position and she pukes over your new trainers.

4. If you get out of your car you'll cause a traffic jam.

5. Once you become involved you'll have to stay with her until the ambulance comes, and you'll have to go to a house nearby and ask

them to make her a cup of sweet tea, then you'll have to sit with her on the pavement with all the fag butts and dog turds, telling her jokes and asking her about the war just to stop her from losing consciousness; then when you're late for work your boss won't believe you because you used the same excuse last week.

6. Old people bruise really badly, and although you're curious to see how she colours up, it will probably be a few hours before they really start to show.

7. There's lots of other people walking past and ignoring her; if any of them stop they'll probably be

doctors, firemen or surgeons, or something.

8. You're worried she'll ask you to go home and feed her scrappy little tartan-wearing dog while she lives it up in casualty.

9. You're late for church.

10. You just ate a big lunch and don't want to be there when the paramedics start cutting off her clothes.

10 REASONS NOT TO GET A DOG

1. Dog hair sticks to everything except the dog.
2. If God had meant us to keep dogs as pets, he wouldn't have invented the Chinese.
3. It makes you jealous when they lick places you can't reach.
4. Your tin opener is broken.
5. A dog costs about £6,000 over its lifetime – the same price as the sound system for your Vauxhall Nova.

6. They eat children, their own poop and anything else in your house that's not nailed down.
7. You start using words like "poop".
8. They lick their balls and then your face.
9. They like to hump furniture.
10. When you're lying on the kitchen floor after taking an overdose, instead of calling an ambulance they chow down on your face.

10 REASONS NOT TO UPDATE YOUR WARDROBE

1. Every twenty years you'll come back into vogue.
2. Burberry and tracky bottoms is a classic look that will always be in fashion.
3. Ditto tassels.
4. As long as you know how to accessorize, it doesn't matter what you wear. A purple scrunchie always makes you look well lush.
5. You choose comfort above style every time – loose clothing makes it easier to shoplift and run away from the police when you get caught.

6. You were wearing big chunky shoes with a thick heel and square toes way before everyone else – on your club foot.

7. Couture culture is for fashionista faggots, whereas a football strip is practical, synthetic, wipe-clean and comes in XXL.

8. You don't want to pay money to become a walking billboard for some designer label and, besides, you can get it for a fraction of the price down the market.

9. Even in winter, a plain off-white T-shirt is the best way to showcase your bitchin' tattoos, which say much more about you than your gear.

10. There's no chance of making fashion blunders if you opt out.

10 REASONS NOT TO GET A CAT

1. A cat costs about £6,000 over its lifetime.
2. It sleeps for 18 hours a day, and you sleep for 8 – do the maths.
3. Do you think it would let you live if it were the size of a lion?
4. It does hairy shits.
5. It can't stop an intruder.
6. It keeps vermin out of the garden, but brings dead carcasses into the house.

7. It lies on its arse all the time waiting to be fed and then pukes up as soon as it has eaten.
8. Only lesbians, witches and old ladies like them.
9. Sixty-five percent of cats are possessed by the Devil.
10. It's a myth that they bury their shit.

5 REASONS NOT TO DONATE ORGANS

1. You don't want your liver or heart ending up in some piss head or heavy smoker who doesn't deserve to outlive you.
2. Also, a serial killer who needs a transplant currently has the same priority as every everyone else, subject to need.
3. Alcoholism is the leading cause of liver failure and it costs about £300,000 to perform a transplant on a wino. However, they shouldn't be denied surgery – cutting off their arms is a great idea.

4. There are plenty of brain dead people in your office who wouldn't miss an organ.

5. When you die if your organs aren't already knackered you won't have lived a full life.

10 REASONS NOT TO VOTE

1. Prisoners aren't allowed.
2. It's a waste of time because the price of petrol, beer and fags still goes up every year.
3. You're an individual and don't follow the herd.
4. You've got more chance of winning the lottery than your vote – 1 in 30 million – making a difference.
5. The Hobbesian social contract is a scam which violates human rights: citizens agree to be governed because it is supposed to rescue

them from the state of nature –
war of all against all – so how come
we bombed Iraq?

6. You hate Thursdays.

7. You would if you could text vote.

8. You don't want to support the
   nanny state – you hate pensioners.

9. All politicians like to beat
   themselves off while wearing
   stockings and suspenders; Stephen
   Milligan just got caught.

10. Politics is show business for ugly
    people.

10 REASONS NOT TO HAVE A WASH

1. You were forced to as a child.
2. You don't want to line the pockets of the soap barons.
3. It's dangerous to take a bath when you're constantly pissed or hung over.
4. You only wash before going to church: Christmas and Easter.
5. Good bacteria eat the bad bacteria.
6. Dirt is a state a mind and you've got a filthy mind.
7. You keep dropping your cell phone in the bath.

8. A bath is just sitting in your own dirty water, and a shower means standing up.
9. You could fall asleep and drown.
10. It's Yom Kippur.

10 REASONS NOT TO GIVE TO CHARITY COLLECTORS

1. Charity begins at home and you need a new widescreen TV.
2. Since the Tsunami you've developed compassion fatigue.
3. You do your bit: you're already heavily committed to taking the stuff you can't sell on eBay to Oxfam.
4. What's the point of saving a starving kid you're never going to meet and who can't even thank you in English?
5. Why does money have to change hands? Every good act is charity.

6. Ninety percent of the money is lost on administration costs – that's pens, biscuits and toilet paper for do-gooders.

7. You already donate £20 each week to the National Lottery Commission.

8. It says in the good book: "Heal the sick, raise the dead, cleanse those who have leprosy, drive out demons. Freely you have received, freely give." You're not qualified to do the first two, and there aren't any lepers or possessed people on your estate.

9. You'd happily donate a blanket, but it won't fit into the collection tin.

10. No matter how disadvantaged someone is, they can always sell drugs.

10 REASONS NOT TO GO TO THE GYM

1. You add one minute of your life for every minute you exercise, so where's the saving?
2. It's more fun being addicted to chocolate than endorphins.
3. You don't want to ruin your new Abercrombie trackie.
4. You skipped breakfast this morning.
5. No pain, no pain.
6. If God meant us to touch our toes, he'd have put them on our knees.
7. It's a waste of calories when there are people starving in Africa.

8. You get plenty of exercise running away from store detectives.
9. The only body part you enjoy developing is your right arm.
10. MTV sucks ass.

10 REASONS NOT TO SHAVE

1. Last time you nearly cut off your balls.
2. None of the other French girls do it.
3. You will, just as soon as somebody gives you a job.
4. Mammals are supposed to be hairy.
5. You're a haemophiliac; one nick and you could bleed out.
6. Shaving causes red bumps and ingrown hair follicles.
7. Your facial hair is a channel of holiness.

8. The Bible forbids it: "Ye shall not round the corners of your heads, neither shalt thou mar the corners of thy beard." (Leviticus 19:27).
9. In a lifetime a man spends 3,300 hours shaving.
10. Shaving removes as much skin as it does hair.

10 REASONS NOT TO BUY A ROUND

1. You lost all your money in the fruit machine.
2. You bought the crisps last time.
3. You forgot to bring your I.D.
4. You're sure you're too pissed – you'll never get served.
5. You're not staying long.
6. You're too short.
7. The beer is warm.
8. The bar is in Sweden, Norway or Japan.
9. You're saving up for a kebab.
10. You're a woman.

5 REASONS NOT TO VISIT SICK RELATIVES IN HOSPITAL

1. You're afraid of catching MRSA.
2. They've already made their will.
3. They're in a coma. You feel like a prat sitting by their bedside stroking their hand and talking crap, when the only thing on your mind is when you can have a smoke.
4. Colostomy bags and papier mâché spittoons.
5. You don't want anyone doing tests on your neck goitre.

10 REASONS NOT TO RECYCLE

1. Who gives a shit about future generations?
2. You don't want to have children, so why should you provide for everybody else's future?
3. You have a right to dispose of your property however you want.
4. Drinking out of a second-hand can is disgusting.
5. We've got plenty of room for landfill. If all the solid waste for the next 1,000 years was put into a single place, it would only take up 40 square miles of space.

6. Recycling paper doesn't save trees. The fewer trees we need, the fewer we'll grow.
7. Recycling is more expensive than landfill, except for aluminium, and it creates its own toxic waste (recycling newspapers uses tonnes of bleach to get rid of the ink).
8. It takes four times more energy to recycle paper than to make it from virgin wood pulp.
9. The recycling agenda is a government ploy to get us to tolerate gradual erosion in our living standards.
10. Recycling means the hippies have won.

10 REASONS NOT TO SEND CHRISTMAS CARDS

1. The whole "Did they send to me last year?" thing is just such a waste of human existence.

2. There's always someone who sends you a card and you haven't sent them one, so you go to the shop and the only thing you can find costs more than your car but you have to buy it because otherwise you'll miss the last post, and then your girlfriend complains because you never spend that much on a card for her, and then you end up getting into an argument and

accidently hitting her, so she goes to stay with her friend, and on Christmas day you have to settle for a frozen pizza and a wank, all because you got sent a card from someone you don't like enough to send one to in the first place.

3. It screws up the postal system for five weeks either side of Christmas so that if you want to send something important it will be delayed because those lazy, thieving bastards at the Royal Mail are too busy steaming open all the cards to steal the postal orders inside.

4. If we didn't provide billions of pounds of revenue each year for the Royal Mail during the festive

period, the company would have to start running an efficient and competitive postal service that justifies the outrageously high postal charges.

5. Nothing says "I don't give a shit about you" better than receiving one of a box of twenty identical Christmas cards containing a poorly written and mawkish inscription. The expensive cards, with the sender's name and address printed in copperplate are even worse, because they mean "I don't give a shit about you, and I also earn more money than you do".

6. If it weren't for Christmas cards, people you hate wouldn't have the

opportunity to send you a round-robin letter boasting about all the great things they've been doing during the year, to remind you how little you've achieved in the last twelve months, like how they've just bought their little virtuoso brat her first Stradivarius and treated themselves to an unassuming little holiday home in Sardinia.

7. It prevents middle class people from giving to charity, because the 0.1p that is donated every time they send one of their fifty miserable little cards salves their consciences for the rest of the year.

8. If all the trees that are chopped down each year to make Christmas

cards were left to grow, global
warming would slow down by
98.3%.

9. When Jesus was born nobody sent
    any cards, and by all accounts it was
    still one of the best Christmases ever.

10. Men are clever enough to realize that
    it's a waste of time but women still
    buy into this commercial con, and
    then criticize them because they are
    the only ones taking part in this
    pointless ritual.

5 REASONS NOT TO BUY YOUR OWN FAGS

1. Every fag you mooch increases someone else's life expectancy.
2. You just quit smoking and if you buy a packet you'll start again.
3. You smoke right down to the filter, so there's less wastage.
4. Mooching is merely a more efficient means of passive smoking.
5. You're saving yourself for your sixteenth birthday.

10 REASONS NOT TO GO TO CHURCH

1. It's full of big-assed hypocrites and smelly pensioners pretending to worship something they don't really believe in, just to show off how holy they are, so they can get into heaven, which doesn't exist, so what a big waste of time that is.

2. If heaven does exist, there are only 144,000 places and they're all reserved for the Jehovah's Witnesses.

3. Most priests and vicars are kiddy-fiddlers.

4. The singing keeps you awake. As does the sexual abuse.
5. You prefer to stay at home reading Leviticus and praying God kills all the homosexuals.
6. Communion wafers are dry as hell and always give you the munchies.
7. Money is the root of all evil, but churches are always asking for it.
8. When you were a kid you always associated church with stopping you from doing more interesting things like opening Christmas presents and eating chocolate bunnies.
9. You always get the urge to scream obscenities or yell "bo-oo-ring" at the top of your voice.

10. Lots of dead people are buried under the floor. It wouldn't be tolerated at McDonald's or Tesco, so why should you be expected to sit in a place of worship knowing that just a few inches beneath your feet are a bunch of corpses?

5 REASONS NOT TO GET OUT OF BED

1. Statistically it's one of the safest places you can spend the day.
2. You've run out of cigarettes and clean thongs.
3. You don't have to sign on until Thursday.
4. It's the only way you won't be tempted to break your ASBO.
5. You can't do anything in the morning until you've had a cup of coffee, a cigarette and gone back to sleep.

10 REASONS NOT TO DONATE BLOOD

1. A pint – that's nearly an armful.
2. You'll miss your appointment at the Hepatitis clinic.
3. Without life-saving blood transfusions 4.5 million Americans would die each year.
4. This morning you got a Prince Albert, a tattoo and then took it up the arse.
5. Donating sperm pays, blood doesn't.
6. You're waiting until after the next 9/11.

7. You're a gay Jehovah's Witness recreational drug user.
8. You can't smoke for two hours afterwards.
9. You're a vegetarian.
10. You do your bit – every month you send your used tampons to the Red Cross.

10 REASONS NOT TO USE DEODORANT

1. It makes it harder to plait your underarm hair.
2. None of the other German girls do it.
3. The smell of your yeast infection disguises your B.O.
4. What's wrong with smelling like a musty ox?
5. You're sandwiched between two hippies on a long haul flight – what's the point?
6. You're under-stretched at work so you don't perspire that much.

7. If God didn't want us to smell he wouldn't have invented Metallica.
8. You're sending the money you save on deodorant to Greenpeace.
9. You work in I.T.
10. There are more important things to think about like the Altonian brain teaser and organizing your blog by stardate.

10 REASONS NOT TO GO TO WORK

1. You hate the sexual harassment in the workplace – you prefer to do it in your spare time.
2. You only get two fifteen-minute smoking breaks each day, which means you have to chain smoke two packets during the evening.
3. You've been on holiday for two weeks and can't face your inbox.
4. Attendance isn't in your job description.
5. You haven't used up all your sick days yet.

6. Reruns of *Cheers* are only shown during working hours.

7. The company cafeteria isn't subsidized.

8. You need to stay at home and clean your guns.

9. You have to take part in an identity parade.

10. There's been a death in the family – your own.

5 REASONS NOT TO USE A HANDKERCHIEF

1. Blowing your nose is unhygienic, whereas ten minutes of rooting is free entertainment that does no one any harm.
2. Eating whatever comes out of your nose builds up the body's defences, a kind of mucoid homeopathy.
3. You wouldn't dream of carrying a turd around in your pocket, and yet many people think nothing of stuffing a germ-ridden rag up their sleeve.

4. Nose blowing is noisy and therefore the most indiscreet way of clearing your tubes.
5. Washing handkerchiefs damages the environment.

10 REASONS NOT TO DO YOGA

1. You found a dead spider on your yoga mat the other day.
2. You can already fellate yourself.
3. It doesn't burn any calories.
4. Heroin is more effective than yoga – you can touch the floor with your elbows and you don't feel a thing.
5. All of the *Star Wars* characters suck.
6. Because yoga teachers always tell you to "breathe the pain through". Screw them, it still hurts like crap.
7. You've never found a yoga class where you can smoke.

8. You can't bear to share a room with a group of double-jointed pretzels in designer leotards.
9. Right now, stress is the only thing stopping you from having a nervous breakdown.
10. Yoga is supposed to combat cravings – but you never lose the craving to stop.

10 REASONS NOT TO GO ON A DIET

1. You prefer to be morbidly obese than look like Gillian McKeith.
2. Why should you lose weight when your partner is such a fat ugly minger?
3. You're American.
4. You've just renewed your season ticket at Dunkin' Donuts.
5. You're frightened you'll discover that you're ugly anyway.
6. If you lost weight you'd have to buy new clothes.

7. Your cats love playing with your jelly rolls.
8. You are currently 535lb and hope to beat the world record soon before you die of congestive heart failure.
9. Your embolism collection is a work in progress.
10. Despite the fact that you can't get laid, you're breathless all the time and you cry yourself to sleep every night, you're PROUD TO BE FAT.

ARE YA' BOVVERED?

10 REASONS NOT TO DO FOREPLAY

1. Humans are the only animals that waste time with it.
2. Doesn't the half hour of pre-coital begging count?
3. You just spent ten minutes unclasping her bra.
4. She can either have foreplay or a cuddle afterwards – she's not getting both.
5. You just bought a gallon jar of Vaseline.
6. You find Rohypnol is the best way to loosen them up.

7. Sheep aren't fussy.
8. Your husband could come home at any time.
9. There's pizza arriving in ten.
10. Exhuming the cadaver usually gets you plenty in the mood.

10 REASONS NOT TO GO TO SCHOOL

1. You don't need qualifications to become Minister for Education.
2. You hate your parents and want them to be sent to prison.
3. School is full of bullying and one-upman ship – and that's just in the staff room.
4. Albert Einstein thought school "strangled the holy curiosity of inquiry" and he did all right.
5. You forget 85% of what you learn in school, so what's the point of learning it in the first place?

6. You've got lots of emotional intelligence. Like, if someone had split up with their boyfriend, they'd come to you to talk about it. You can't teach that at school.

7. You don't want to be a disruptive influence in class.

8. Fifty-five thousand school kids bunk off each year and the government has spent £885 million trying to fix the problem. So if you truant your share should be about sixteen grand.

9. Learning is a two-way process, but the teachers just don't seem to want to learn from you.

10. Your dad told you that bunking off will make you an official figure.

10 REASONS NOT TO QUIT SMOKING

1. You've got private healthcare insurance.
2. You love it too much to develop the desire to stop.
3. You've always fancied getting a tracheotomy.
4. Smoking takes ten years off your life – the worse years – the ones at the end.
5. Quitting is easy – you've done it loads of times already.
6. Everyone quits smoking in the end.

7. Wheezing when you walk up stairs is a better alternative to feeling fit and homicidal.
8. You only feel like you're really living when you're killing yourself.
9. You got a Zippo for your birthday.
10. Only smokers who haven't quit still hold the power to improve their chances of living so dramatically.

10 REASONS NOT TO OBEY THE SPEED LIMIT

1. All speed is relative.
2. It's cars that kill, not speed.
3. It's impossible to go slow when you're listening to Eminem.
4. There's no speed limit on German autobahns, and they're the most uptight nation in the world.
5. Your girlfriend is going to give birth (in about five months).
6. The police are chasing you and you've already thrown your Bull Mastiff out of the window.

7. You need to escape a pursuing photographer who is driving dangerously.
8. You want to test your advanced driving skills.
9. You have diarrhoea.
10. You're being tailgated by Kenneth Noye.

10 REASONS NOT TO MAKE POVERTY HISTORY

1. You haven't collected all the bracelets yet.
2. All those starving people in Africa just sit around all day attracting flies instead of getting off their arses to dig some latrines.
3. All that jumping in the air for BBC idents is a waste of calories.
4. Global warming is going to flood most of India and Africa within 20 years – end of problem.
5. Gandhi didn't eat much and you never heard him complain.

6. Live Aid concerts are the only time you get to hear Boy George sing these days.
7. "Make Poverty Cool" would be easier and much more popular.
8. It's just another excuse for George Bush and Tony Blair to have man sex.
9. Rich nations rely on the outsourcing of cheap labour and raw materials from the poorest.
10. White millionaire popstars and benevolent capitalists poncing around makes you want to puke into your cup of fair trade coffee.

10 REASONS NOT TO WIPE YOUR ARSE

1. If you're eating a healthy diet, you shouldn't need to.
2. You're going to the swimming pool later.
3. You're a one-armed Muslim.
4. You can't decide whether to wipe standing or sitting.
5. Your bidet has broken and you've forgotten how to do it the old-fashioned way.
6. Your girlfriend just dumped you.
7. Your anal fistula just burst.
8. It's your butler's day off.

9. You can't be bothered to unzip your wetsuit.
10. You're late for work.

10 REASONS NOT TO SAVE A STRANDED WHALE

1. We don't need another national faux melodrama; Diana's funeral was bad enough.
2. Let nature take its course. Any animal stupid enough to get beached deserves to die.
3. Only the British could look a gift horse in the mouth when seven tonnes of sushi swims ashore.
4. They should be killed and the blubber used to make scented candles.
5. The money spent on saving it could be put to better use – such as whaling.

6. If whales (according to a fourteenth-century statute) are classed as "fishes royal", why should you pay to rescue one of the Queen's pets? She should foot the bill. In Henry VIII's time it would have been stuffed with dolphins and spit-roasted.

7. It should have been left in the Thames, raising the stakes on the Varsity boat race.

8. Whales are fat and bald. Shoot it in the face.

9. A big fish is still a fish, just like a big turd is still a turd.

10. If we just let all the stupid whales swim up the Thames and die, then maybe it would eliminate this annoying trait from the gene pool.

10 REASONS NOT TO STOP SMACKING YOUR KIDS

1. Physical violence has always been a sublimely expressive way of administering discipline.
2. It's OK to give them a good lathering so long as you explain why you're doing it, e.g. "You've been a naughty little shit."
3. If they're going to hate your guts when they grow up, you may as well give them a good reason.
4. It's best to get some good beatings in before they outgrow you.

5. As long as you are consistent with your larruping, it's OK. Children only become unhappy if they don't know the routine.

6. It's a great way to vent your anger.

7. Scandinavians aren't allowed to lay into their offspring, and they have the highest suicide rates in the world.

8. "Do not withhold discipline from a child; if you punish him with the rod, he will not die. Punish him with the rod and save his soul from death." (Proverbs 23:13-14).

9. Fifty years ago millions of people were brought up on a good whupping and they didn't all turn into parent killers.

10. Life is a house of pain, and you're just teaching them an early lesson.

10 REASONS NOT TO CLEAN UP WHEN YOUR DOG SHITS ON THE PAVEMENT

1. It's biodegradable and, anyway, your dog always craps in the corner of the pavement.
2. You've got a tiny dog that doesn't produce nearly as much crap as a Labrador or Great Dane.
3. You pay your taxes so that menials can sweep the streets – it's not your job.

4. Carrying around a Tesco bag full of crap until you can find a bin is demeaning and very uncool.

5. And anyway, all the local shit bins have been burnt by little cretins so many times that the council has stopped replacing them.

6. You are always stepping in dog shit, so why should you clean up when other people don't?

7. It's either going to rain later or be a hot day, so the turd will be washed away or biscuit-dry-safe soon.

8. If it gives kids worms or makes them blind then their parents should stop them from eating shit and rubbing it in their eyes, and buy them some proper toys.

9. The police don't care; they're too busy playing with their fascist speeding guns and murdering innocent Brazilians.

10. What's your dog supposed to do – hold it in forever?

5 REASONS NOT TO GET MARRIED

1. There's a just impediment – you're still shagging your fiancée's sister.
2. Nobody's pregnant, so what's the hurry?
3. The only time you make speeches is in court.
4. Bigamy is illegal.
5. You're saving up for another sovvy.

10 REASONS NOT TO ALLOW YOUR KIDS TO BELIEVE IN SANTA

1. You spend all year telling them to beware of strangers, but it's OK for a 350lb geriatric prick in a red jump suit to sneak around their bedroom while they're asleep.
2. No white dude would come into your neighbourhood after dark.
3. There's no way that those reindeer could fly fast enough to get him around the world in one evening, even allowing for time zones and the rotation of the earth.

4. You want your kids to appreciate that you are the one who worked your arse off all year so you could pay for all their crap.

5. When they grow up and start working in Burger King you don't want them to hate you for lying to them and fooling them into believing there is any magic in this miserable world.

6. The sooner you get the whole Santa/Easter Bunny/Tooth Fairy thing out in the open, the sooner you can explain that God doesn't exist and there's no afterlife.

7. They shouldn't learn to be good all year for material gain; instead they should learn that's it's the best way

to avoid having the crap beaten out of them.

8. Letting your kids believe all that nonsense is the best way to ensure they get the crap beaten out of them at school as well.

9. Believing in Santa is so gay and so are his reindeer, especially Rudolph.

10. Santa is a bad role model. Your kids should be taught that anyone who gives without expecting anything in return is a pussy. So either he doesn't exist or he's got an ulterior motive for hiding candy in their socks – now what do you think that could be, eh kids?

5 REASONS NOT TO GET AN IPOD

1. After you've got bored of listening to your five-star playlist, you start thinking you've got crap musical taste.
2. £400 is too much to spend on a portable music player when you can pick up a Walkman on eBay for £1.50
3. Steve Jobs is shagging your girlfriend.
4. iPod socks don't come in Burberry check.
5. They've all sold out, again.

10 REASONS NOT TO TIP IN A RESTAURANT

1. Most waiters and waitresses are actors who earn a shit load during the day doing adverts and Hollywood films, while you have to work for a living.

2. Why should you pay someone ten percent of the cost of your already overpriced meal just for carrying a plate from the kitchen to your table? Even a retarded monkey could do that.

3. They put on their fake smiles and use all sorts of tricks just so you'll leave them a big fat tip; the worst is

when they squat so that their faces are at eye level and they think that makes them appear all friendly and approachable, when it really just makes them look like pricks. If those same staff were working in a snooty Mayfair restaurant they'd treat you like a walking piece of dog shit, so screw them.

4. Another tactic is to tell you their name: "Hello, I'm Dan and I'll be your waiter this evening." Like you give a shit. Look, dickwad, just bring me the food and keep your personal problems to yourself, OK pal?

5. And what about when they draw smiley faces on the bill, like that's

going to make you hand over a bunch of notes? How old do they think you are? Four?

6. Those fascist scabs would be the first to rugby tackle you if you did a runner without paying the bill.

7. You shouldn't be held to ransom just in case they spit in your food. You're the customer – after the meal you should get to decide whether or not they keep their jobs. That would keep them on their toes and discourage them from hocking up in your soup.

8. China may have one of the most repressive regimes in the world but at least it's got one thing right – tipping is illegal.

9. It's hard enough working out how to split the bill without worrying about subsidizing minimum-wage earners.

10. If they want tips they should go work in a strip club.

10 REASONS NOT TO LEARN A FOREIGN LANGUAGE

1. English is the global lingua franca (apart from Mandarin).
2. Foreign languages contain weird sounds and gestures like throat clearing (Welsh, Arabic, etc.), biting your thumb (Italian), pouting (French), shrugging (French again) and pretending not to understand when someone attempts to speak your piss-poor parochial little language (French again).

3. Lots of languages have pointless genders for stuff, like calling a loaf of bread female. It's not alive; it doesn't have breasts (baps excluded) or independent thoughts, for Christ's sake.

4. Many languages steal English words because foreigners are too lazy to think up their own (especially the Welsh and the French).

5. A head butt is the most effective way of breaking down cultural barriers.

6. It is well known that when you speak another tongue you start thinking like a foreigner, so say you learn French you end up believing that it is acceptable to shit through

a hole in the floor rather than sit on a toilet; or you try German and soon you find Mr Bean funny and think that tennis players with transparent eyebrows, taking seven minutes to pour a pint of beer and changing your national borders every fifty years is perfectly normal.

7. Unless you're living abroad, learning the language is artificial and boring. You learn stuff like "the monkey is underneath the table" rather than useful phrases like "Where is the fish and chip shop?" or "Do you swallow?"

8. When a foreigner speaks English badly, do you respect him for trying, or do you just think he's a

retard and wish he would stop saying "errrr" every two seconds? That's what you sound like when you speak foreign.

9. You can't understand foreign sober, let alone when you're pissed.

10. Wherever you are in the world you can communicate with the locals by singing loudly and throwing chairs.

10 REASONS NOT TO GIVE UP YOUR SEAT ON A BUS TO A PREGNANT WOMAN

1. Who else is going to drive?
2. Bed rest used to be the misguided and very dangerous advice given to pregnant women. You don't want to compound the errors of the past by letting her take the weight off her feet.
3. Do what is best for the baby, which, by the way, is floating in a sack of phlegm inside her womb

and doesn't give a shit whether the mother is sitting down or bungee jumping from the Clifton suspension bridge.

4. Pregnancy is natural, but giving up your seat is not.

5. She should have thought about her public transport requirements before she got herself knocked up.

6. You're fatter and more breathless than her.

7. Swollen ankles are all part of the magical tapestry of pregnancy.

8. She's so ugly she should just be thankful she found someone to shag her, and now she wants your seat, too?

9. You don't want the driver to see you sniffing glue.
10. The explosives strapped to your chest weigh twice as much as a baby.

5 REASONS NOT TO PAY FOR STUFF

1. Store detectives are too fat to catch you.
2. If it weren't for shoplifting, they would have to work in McDonald's.
3. All property is theft, even the stuff you pay for.
4. You'll be punished in heaven.
5. You believe in the free-market.

10 REASONS NOT TO GIVE TO BUSKERS

1. Today the kids are with your ex-wife so you have absolutely no reason to stop so the little brats can make friends with the untalented drop-out roaring *Wonderwall* so tunelessly you seriously consider ripping his throat open so that you can count the nodules on his vocal chords.

2. They are the scourge of every city, ranking just below pigeons – often the boundary is blurred, since they both deserve a good kicking.

3. It's begging for untalented adenoidal pricks who can't juggle, eat fire or ride a unicycle.

4. They are a fire hazard. When you are in an Underground emergency, you like to know that you can beat everyone to the escalators without having to trample a sad loser who should have been put out of his misery years ago.

5. The worst ones are the middle class music students who play in groups of two or three, and have music stands and all that faggoty shit, and get so much cash they have to call their rich parents to come and collect them. Even more reason to give them a good kicking.

6. They have the audacity to try to sell you their homemade CD. Oasis were shit the first time round; if you liked them you'd have bought *Definitely Maybe* in 1994 and got even more whining nasal banality for your buck.

7. They can't even get an open-mike gig in a pub or club so they decide to peddle their musical graffiti to demonstrate just why they can't get a booking.

8. They either suck or they're showing off, and there's nothing in between. You hate them for being shit, but you also hate them for being too good, like the ones who

can play the Sibelius violin concerto on one string (music students again, most likely – get the boot in before daddy arrives in his Merc).

9. At least beggars are honest – they just ask for your money, without pretending that they have the talent to entertain you in return.

10. They go down really easily in a fight and whimper like girls even before you have kicked them in the head.

ARE YA' BOVVERED?

10 REASONS NOT TO APPRECIATE CLASSICAL MUSIC

1. No one has ever lost their virginity to Brahms's D-Minor Piano Concerto.
2. It's dead music for dead white rich old people, the sort of hi-brow bores who have hifi systems that appear out of the wall when they fart but don't have any visible means of operating them at all.
3. It sounds great in car commercials, but it's not something you'd listen to for pleasure.

4. You've tooled up your car with sub-woofers; it just doesn't cater for those faggoty high frequencies.

5. Bling and Beethoven just don't go together.

6. If you wanted to slit your wrists you'd listen to Joy Division.

7. You shouldn't have to "learn" to appreciate any music.

8. When earth mother mental defectives play tunes to their baby in the womb, it's always classical music that they choose – proof that it's elitist and recherché bollocks.

9. Most classical composers were deaf or consumptive retards who couldn't get a proper job.

10. You don't like the dress code.

10 REASONS NOT TO SEE SOMEONE ELSE'S POINT OF VIEW

1. Empathy is merely accommodating someone else's self-interest.
2. Listening is overrated. The only social lubricant you need belongs in a tube in your bathroom.
3. Fear, not consensus, is the foundation for morality.
4. Every conflict can be resolved two ways: by violence or the threat of it.

5. Someone else's views form a focus group of one.

6. Great leaders listen to the voices in their head.

7. It's easier to ask for forgiveness than permission.

8. If they don't have a gun they don't get your attention.

9. If you walk a mile in someone else's shoes you'll either get blisters or athlete's foot.

10. If other people minded their own bloody business, there wouldn't be so much hate in the world.

10 REASONS NOT TO STOP AFTER HITTING SOMEONE WITH YOUR CAR

1. It's a rough neighbourhood, and you don't want to risk getting mugged.
2. You're approaching top speed; it would be a shame not to see what this baby can do.
3. It looks like you killed him, so there's no point putting him into the recovery position or saying sorry.

4. You haven't got room in your trunk for another body.

5. You don't need to notify the police – it looks like the victim's partner already radioed for backup.

6. The hill is a one in four and you need all the momentum your 1.2 litre engine can muster.

7. You've still got plenty of beer left on the front seat.

8. You've got to get to the body shop for a re-spray and change of windscreen before your parents gets home.

9. Your starter motor is playing up.

10. You don't want to cause an accident.

10 REASONS NOT TO TAKE YOUR MEDICATION

1. You're too depressed.
2. You will just as soon as you've cleaned up the blood and hidden the body.
3. You only do what the voices tell you.
4. The prophylactics don't work – you may as well shove them up your arse.
5. Manic laughter is the best medicine.
6. What's the point? They won't have time to take effect before your body hits the pavement.

7.   You're trying acupuncture, on your neighbour, with a bread knife.

8.   You're not ill, and you'll kill the next person who says you're psychotic.

9.   The side effects are really unpleasant, such as the ability to return to work.

10. Killing people makes you feel calmer than any drug.

10 REASONS NOT TO LOVE HUMANITY

1. Fifty percent of people are below average intelligence.
2. The world was perfect when you created it, but the combined efforts of humanity and the Devil have destroyed it.
3. Not enough people have made the switch to contact lenses.
4. The fact that a Swedish chain saw manufacturer had to stick a warning label on their products saying "Do not attempt to stop chain with your hands or genitals".

5. They just hurt you; they're scum.
    You want to make them hurt back
    and go away forever.

6. You don't hate humanity, just
    people.

7. In fact, it's mostly the stupid, ugly
    ones you hate, especially the
    unsightly sons of bitches who
    maintain that real beauty is on the
    inside.

8. It always seems to be the stupid
    ones who get to run everything.

9. Society has become too forgiving.
    Plato was right when he advocated
    that human reproduction should be
    controlled by government.

10. You pay for 512K broadband and
    only get 500K.

10 REASONS NOT TO STAY SOBER

1. Visiting in-laws, maxed-out credit cards, three children, dead-end job, the endless grind – how many reasons do you need?
2. The only meaningful ritual in your life is taking your premium sommelier corkscrew out of its box and hacking away at the screw cap of yet another bottle of Jack Daniels.
3. Tequila shots contain powerful anti-oxidants.

4. You live for the nights you'll never remember with the friends you'll never forget.
5. Since you lost your license, it's the only way you can get up enough courage to drive.
6. You prefer to drink your calories than eat them.
7. You can have sex with fat hairy girls for hours without jizzing.
8. It makes living in a caravan and being on the dole more bearable.
9. It's always happy hour somewhere.
10. If you didn't drink, somebody else would.

5 REASONS NOT TO PAY TAXES

1. You always catch the bus, innit?
2. Social security benefit is taxed at source.
3. Because it's only wasted on boring stuff like schools and roads.
4. Either you can lose 30% of your income through taxation, or stop paying taxes and let the national currency lose 30% of its value through inflation. In either case your buying power would be the same.

5. You just turned your bedroom into a tax-haven by declaring it an independent country.

5 REASONS NOT TO HAVE A HEALTH CHECK—UP

1. Doctors are hypocrites – they even have to take a hypocritical oath before they're allowed to work.
2. Your doctor always takes your temperature with his finger.
3. You know you're dying from something the medical profession has never seen before, but you don't want a disease named after you.
4. All the smart kids you bullied at school became doctors.

5. You can diagnose yourself from the letters page of women's magazines, so who needs doctors?

10 REASONS NOT TO BRUSH YOUR TEETH

1. You prefer to spend the extra two minutes in bed.
2. You never eat apples anyway.
3. Flouride is a poison that causes premature ageing and it is a by-product of the manufacture of atomic bombs. Most countries have banned fluoridation in water, but they still put it in toothpaste.
4. You don't want to look like an American.
5. Animals don't need to brush their teeth, so why should we?

6. Your boss doesn't pay you enough to smile.
7. There are only three occasions you put anything in your mouth – eating, smoking and sex.
8. Your teeth are so yellow you just scrape them with a penknife.
9. All that effort for six lumps of enamel?
10. The batteries for your electric toothbrush are in your MP3 player.

5 REASONS NOT TO PLAY WITH YOUR KIDS

1. The restraining order.
2. Ignoring them fosters independence.
3. You have more sophisticated tastes than shoplifting, shooting air guns at horses and poking road kill with a stick.
4. You have to walk the dog.
5. You don't want to over-stimulate them; they're already hyperactive.

5 REASONS NOT TO BREASTFEED YOUR BABY

1. Nungers are sexual objects that are wasted on babies and should instead be treated with the awed reverence which they deserve.

2. It isn't natural, otherwise women wouldn't have to learn how to do it and they wouldn't get cracked and bleeding nipples.

3. When you're breastfeeding you can't have sex, drink alcohol, caffeine or take prescription medication.

4. Smug lactating earth mothers who won't stop talking about La Leche League.
5. It makes female babies grow up lesbian and male babies become nipple-fixated mummy's boys.

5 REASONS NOT TO EAT TOFU

1. It looks like squares of furniture padding foam.
2. It tastes like squares of furniture padding foam.
3. It is more expensive than squares of furniture padding foam.
4. _____
   (add your own reason here).
5. _____
   (add your own reason here).

5 REASONS NOT TO HOLD IN YOUR FARTS

1. The gases can build up inside and poison your blood.
2. Next to wanking, cutting the cheese is the most fun you can have without involving another person or spending money.
3. You're sulphate intolerant.
4. Your sex life imploded years ago, so what difference does it make?
5. When you're sitting on a vinyl seat, holding on is such a missed opportunity.

5 REASONS NOT TO BE MONOGAMOUS

1. Monogamy sucks monkey privates; it drains you of your soul, killing you slowly day by day until you struggle to remember what it was like to feel the thrill of a spontaneous sexual urge.

2. In what other area of your life do you stick to having just one of something? You have two cars, seven shirts, twelve pairs of socks, two televisions, three meals a day and snacks in between. Why should a relationship be any different?

3. Imagine choosing to shag the same person for the rest of your life, nobody else, ever, until you die. Do you think in heaven you get rewarded for your self-sacrifice with an eternal shagfest? Not likely. If heaven exists then you can bet that vanilla male-female monogamy will be the only option available.

4. All war and hatred on earth is made by people who don't get enough.

5. Monogamy is a social imposition peddled to us by corrupt serial adulterer politicians seeking to deny the rest of us an authentic sexual response.

ARE YA'

BOVVERED?

If you have enjoyed this book,
please see others like it on
www.crombiejardine.com

All Crombie Jardine books are available from High
Street bookshops, Amazon or Bookpost
(P.O. Box 29, Douglas, Isle of Man, IM99 1BQ.
Tel: 01624 677237, Fax: 01624 670923,
Email: bookshop@enterprise.net.
Postage and packing free within the UK).